Exclusive Distributors:
Music Sales Limited
8/9 Frith Street,
London W1V 5TZ, England.

Music Sales Pty Limited
120 Rothschild Avenue,
Rosebery, NSW 2018,
Australia.

Order No. AM955328
ISBN 0-7119-7486-1
This book © Copyright 1999
by Wise Publications
www.internetmusicshop.com

Designed by
CDT Design.

Music processed by
Paul Ewers Music Design.

Printed in Malta by Interprint Limited

Your Guarantee of Quality:
As publishers, we strive to produce
every book to the highest commercial
standards. This book has been carefully
designed to minimise awkward page
turns and to make playing from it a
real pleasure.

Particular care has been given to
specifying acid-free, neutral-sized paper
made from pulps which have not been
elemental chlorine bleached. This pulp is
from farmed sustainable forests and was
produced with special regard for the
environment. Throughout, the printing
and binding have been planned to
ensure a sturdy, attractive publication
which should give years of enjoyment.
If your copy fails to meet our high
standards, please inform us and
we will gladly replace it.

Music Sales' complete catalogue describes
thousands of titles and is available in full
colour sections by subject, direct from
Music Sales Limited. Please state your
areas of interest and send a cheque/postal
order for £1.50 for postage to:
Music Sales Limited, Newmarket Road,
Bury St. Edmunds, Suffolk IP33 3YB.

A Whiter Shade Of Pale

Words & Music by Keith Reid & Gary Brooker

G   Em   G⁷

I was feel - ing kind of sea - sick,
But I wan - dered through my play - ing cards

C   Am Em F

but the crowd called_ out for more,
and would not_ let her be.   the room was hum - ming
               One of six - teen ves - tal

Dm   G   Em G⁷

hard - er   as the ceil - ing flew a - way._
vir - gins   who were leav - ing for the coast,_

C   Am   Em

When we called out for an - oth - - - er drink
and al - tho' my eyes were op - - - en

Barbara Ann

Words & Music by Fred Fassert

-in' and a reel-in' Bar - b'ra Ann, Ba - Ba - Ba - Ba - b'ra Ann.

D.C.al Coda

⊕ Coda

Repeat to fade

-Ba - b'ra Ann. Ba - b'ra Ann, Ba - b'ra Ann. __

Alfie

Words by Hal David. Music by Burt Bacharach

Very slowly, rubato

What's it all a-bout, Al-fie? ___ Is it just for the mo-ment we live? What's it all a-bout ___ when you sort it out, ___ Al-fie? ___

Are we meant to take more than we give, or are we meant to be kind? ___ And if on-ly fools are kind, Al - fie, ___ then I guess it is wise to be cruel. And if life be-longs ___ on-ly to the strong, ___ Al - fie, ___ what will you lend on an old gold-en rule? As

11

Bridal March

By Richard Wagner

Moderato con moto (♩ = c.104)

Bring Me Sunshine

Words by Sylvia Dee. Music by Arthur Kent

See block lyrics for Verse 2

1. Bring me sun-shine___ in your smile,___ bring me laugh-ter___ all the while.___ In this

world where we live, there should be more hap - pi - ness.___

___ So much joy you can give to each brand new bright to - mor -

- row! Make me hap - py ___ through the years.___

Ne - ver bring me ___ an - y tears.___

Let your arms be as warm as the sun from up a-bove,

bring me fun,___ bring me sun - shine, bring me love.

2. Bring me love._____

Verse 2:

Bring me sunshine in your eyes,
Bring me rainbows from the skies.
Life's too short to be spent having anything but fun.
We can be so content if we gather little sunbeams.
Be lighthearted all day long,
Keep me singing happy songs.
Let your arms be as warm as the sun from up above,
Bring me fun, bring me sunshine, bring me love.

Climb Ev'ry Mountain

Words by Oscar Hammerstein II. Music by Richard Rodgers

Maestoso

CHORUS (with deep feeling, like a prayer)

Climb ev - 'ry moun - tain, search high and low,

fol - low ev - 'ry by - way, ev - 'ry path you know.

EastEnders

By Leslie Osborne & Simon May

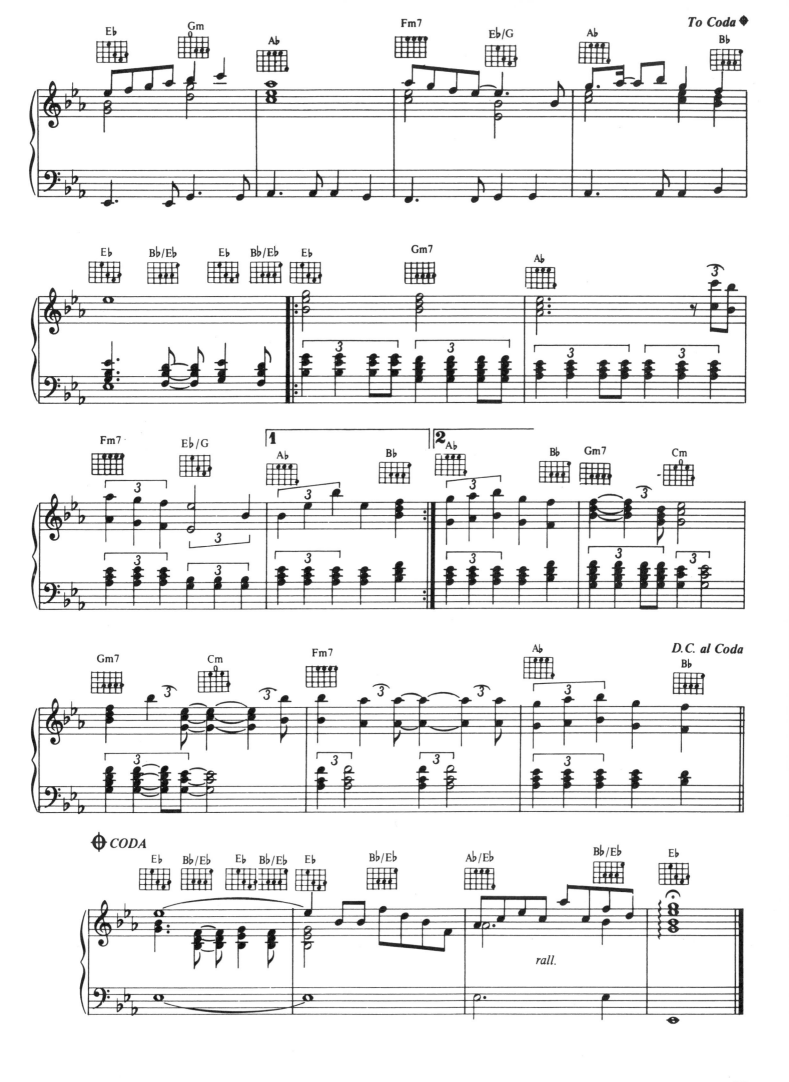

Edelweiss

Words by Oscar Hammerstein II. Music by Richard Rodgers

(Everything I Do) I Do It For You

Words by Bryan Adams & Robert John 'Mutt' Lange. Music by Michael Kamen

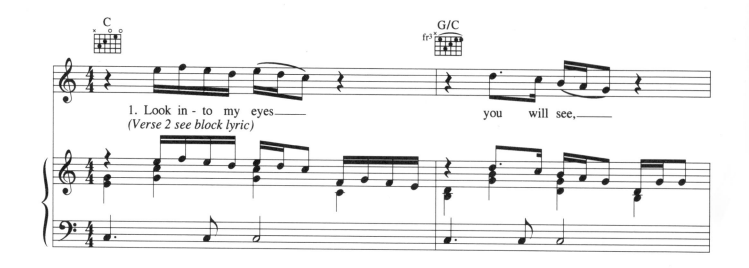

tell me it's not worth try-in' for, you can't tell me it's not worth dy - in'

for. You know it's true,_____ ev-ery-thing I do, I do it for—

you.

1. **2.**

There's

no love like your love and no oth - er could give

more—— love, there's no-where———— un-less you're there all the

time,——————————— all the way—— yeah.——————

1. **2.**

Oh you can't

tell me it's not worth fight-ing for, I can't help— it, there's no-thin' I want more. Yeah— I would

Verse 2:
Look into your heart
You will find there's nothin' there to hide
Take me as I am, take my life
I would give it all, I would sacrifice.

Don't tell me it's not worth fightin' for
I can't help it, there's nothin' I want more
You know it's true, everything I do
I do it for you.

29

Don't Cry For Me Argentina

Music by Andrew Lloyd Webber. Lyrics by Tim Rice

2. I had to let it hap-pen, I had to change; could-n't stay all my life down at heel: Look-ing out of the win-dow, stay-ing out of the sun. So I chose free-dom, run-ning a-round try-ing ev-'ry-thing new, but no-thing im-pressed me at all, I nev-er ex-pect-ed it to.

Slow Tango feel

Tempo 1°

CHORUS

Don't cry for me Ar- gen - ti - na,___ the truth is I nev - er left you: All through my

wild days, my mad ex - ist -ence, I kept my pro -mise, don't keep your

dis - tance.___ Have I said too much? There's no -thing more I can think of to

colla voce

say to you.   But all you have to do is look at me to know that ev - 'ry word is true.

Georgia On My Mind

Words by Stuart Gorrell. Music by Hoagy Carmichael

Goodbye To Love

Words by John Bettis. Music by Richard Carpenter

Goodnight Sweetheart

Words & Music by Ray Noble, Jimmy Campbell & Reg Connelly

Here's That Rainy Day

Words & Music by Johnny Burke & Jimmy Van Heusen

Slowly with expression

How Deep Is Your Love

Words & Music by Barry Gibb, Robin Gibb & Maurice Gibb

I Believe

Words & Music by Ervin Drake, Irvin Graham, Jimmy Shirl & Al Stillman

Moderately (with much expression)

Lyrics:
I Believe for ev - 'ry drop of rain that falls, ___ a flow - er grows. ___ I Be - lieve that some where in the dark - est night, ___ a can - dle glows. ___

heard. _____ I Be-lieve that some-one in the great some-where _____ hears ev-'ry word. _____ Ev-'ry time I hear a new-born ba-by cry, _____ or touch a leaf, _____ or see the sky, _____ then I know why I Be-lieve! _____

Jerusalem

Words by William Blake. Music by Hubert Parry

I Left My Heart In San Francisco

Words by Douglas Cross. Music by George Cory

climb half-way to the stars, _____ the morn-ing

fog _____ may chill the air, I don't

care! My love was there in San Fran-

cis-co, _____ a-bove the blue _____

I Will Always Love You

Words & Music by Dolly Parton

Slow

If

I sweet should stay; mem - o - ries, I would that's all I on - ly be in am tak - ing your with

way, me; so I'll good - bye, go, but I please don't I know cry, I'll we think both

Recite:
I hope that life treats you kind,
and I hope you have all that you ever dreamed of,
and I wish you joy and happiness,
but above all this, I wish you love.

Sing:
And I will always love you,
I will always love you,
I will always love you,
And I will always love you,
I will always love you,
I will always love you.

I Wish You Love

Music & Original Lyrics by Charles Trenet. English Lyrics by Albert A. Beach

Largo (from "The New World")

By Antonin Dvorák

Londonderry Air

Traditional Irish Melody

Slowly

mf *f*

B♭7 E♭ 6fr.

Would God I were the ten- der ap - ple

A♭ 4fr. E♭ 6fr. F7 Fm7 B♭7

blos - som ____ that floats and falls from off the twist- ed bough, ____ to lie and

E♭ 6fr. A♭ 4fr. A♭m 4fr. E♭ 6fr. B♭7

faint with- in your silk- en bo- som, with- in your silk- en bo - - som, as that does

now. _____ Or would I were a lit-tle bur-nished ap - ple _____ for you to pluck me, glid-ing by so cold, _____ while sun and shade your robe of lawn will dap - ple, _____ your robe of lawn _ and your hair's _ spun _ gold. _____

dim. e rit.

Love Me With All Your Heart
(Cuando Calienta El Sol)

Original Words by Mario Rigual. Music by Carlos Rigual & Carlos A. Martinoli. English Words by Michael Vaughn

Just pro-mise me this: ___ that you'll give me ___ all your kiss-es, ___ Ev-'ry

win-ter, ___ ev-'ry sum-mer, ___ ev-'ry fall.

When we are far a-part ___ or when you're near me, ___

Love me with all of your heart as I love you;

Memories Are Made Of This

Words & Music by Terry Gilkyson, Richard Dehr & Frank Miller

Don't for - get a small moon - beam
With some bless-ings from a - bove

Fold in light- ly with a dream.
Serve it gen-'rous-ly with love.

Your lips and mine, Two sips of wine, Mem - or -
One man, one wife, One love thro' life, Mem - or -

ies are made of this.
ies are made of this.

To Coda

Then add the

Men Of Harlech

Welsh Traditional Song

Mona Lisa

Words & Music by Jay Livingston & Ray Evans

In a vil - la in a lit - tle old I - tal - ian town lives a girl whose beau - ty shames the rose. Man - y yearn to love her but their hopes all tum - ble down What does she want? No one knows! Mo - na

this your way to hide a bro-ken heart? Man - y dreams have been brought to your

door - step. They just lie there, and they die there. Are you

warm, are you real, Mo - na Li - sa, or just a

cold and lone - ly, love - ly work of art? Mo - na art?

Moon River

Words by Johnny Mercer. Music by Henry Mancini

Nessun Dorma (from "Turandot")

By Giacomo Puccini

-prà! No, no, sol la tua boc - - ca lo di - rò———— quan - do la

lu - - ce splen - de - rà!———— Ed il mio

ba - cio scioglie - rà il si - len - zio———— che ti fa mi - a!

Di - le - gua, o not - te! Tra - mon - ta - te, stel - le! tra - mon - ta - te,

stel - le! Al - l'al - ba vin - ce - rò! Vin - ce - rò! Vin - ce - rò!

O Sole Mio

Words by Giovanni Capurro. Music by Edorado di Capua

The whole world ov - er,_____ I have searched for some - one,
Too soon the sun - rise,_____ will a - wake the morn - ing,

My search is through, Flor -ence in you to - night.
Then you must go, leav - ing me so a - lone.

Chorus

Night -time in Flor - ence_____ is my de - light,_____

_____ The moon is shin - ing _____ for me to - night. _____

91

Stars twin - kle ____ so high a - bove, ____

Night-time in Flor - ence ____ is time for

love. ____ (2) Stay with me love. ____

Plaisir D'Amour

By Giovanni Paolo Martini

The joy of

love _____ comes on - ly to ___ de - part, ____ it's

sor - - rows bit - ter through ___ a life - - time

prove. I gave up all ___ for cru - el

Syl - via's love. Too soon I found an - oth - er

Raindrops Keep Falling On My Head

Words by Hal David. Music by Burt Bacharach

Rhythmically

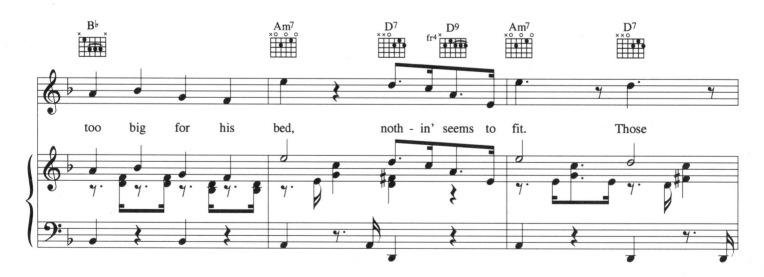

thing I know____ the blues____ they send____ to meet

____ me won't de - feat____ me. It won't be long____ till

hap - pi - ness____ steps up____ to greet____ me.____

Rain - drops keep fall - in' on my head, but

that does-n't mean my eyes will soon be turn-in' red. Cry-in's not for me 'cause I'm nev-er gon-na stop the rain by com-plain-in'. Be - cause I'm free noth-in's wor-ry-in' me.

Scotland The Brave

Traditional Scottish Melody

Sing

Words & Music by Joe Raposo

Moderately

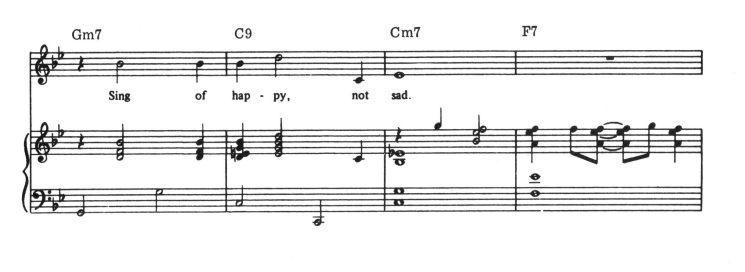

Sing of hap - py, not sad.

Sing! Sing a song. Make it

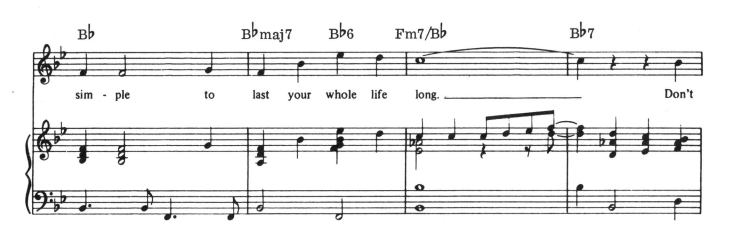

sim - ple to last your whole life long. Don't

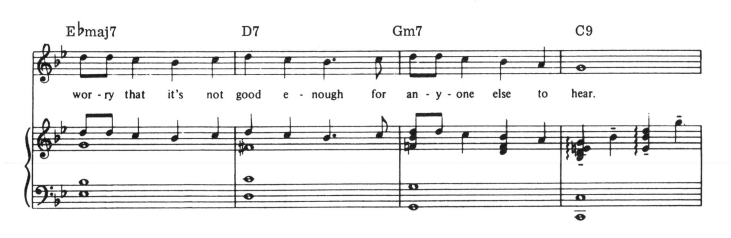

wor - ry that it's not good e - nough for an - y - one else to hear.

Sing!   Sing a song! _____

La la do la da, La da la do la da, La da da la do la da. _____

La do la da, La da la lada, Lo da da la do lo da. _____

Repeat and fade

La la do la da, La da la do la da, La da da la do la da. _____

Repeat and fade

Spanish Eyes

Words by Charles Singleton & Eddie Snyder. Music by Bert Kaempfert

Moderato

1. Blue Span - ish eyes,

(Verse 2 see block lyric)

tear-drops are fall - ing from your Span - ish eyes.

Please, _____ please don't cry _____

this is just a - dios and not good - bye. _____

Soon _____ I'll re - turn _____

bring-ing you all the love your heart can hold. _____

Verse 2:
Blue Spanish eyes
Prettiest eyes in all of Mexico
True Spanish eyes
Please smile for me once more before I go.

Soon I'll return *etc*.

Speak Softly Love
(Love Theme from "The Godfather")

By Nino Rota

Lyrics:

Speak soft-ly, love, and hold me warm a-gainst your heart. I feel your words, the ten-der, trem-bling mo-ments start. We're in a world our ver-y own, shar-ing a love that on-ly few have ev-er known. Wine col-ored

Strangers In The Night

Words by Charles Singleton & Eddie Snyder. Music by Bert Kaempfert

through._____ Some-thing in your eyes_____ was so in - vi -ting,

some-thing in your smile_____ was so ex - ci -ting, some-thing in my heart_____ told me I must have

you._____ Stran -gers in the night,_____ two lone -ly peo -ple, we were

stran -gers in the night,_____ up to the mo -ment when we said our first hel -lo,

Telstar

By Joe Meek

The Can Can

By Jacques Offenbach

The Song From Moulin Rouge (Where Is Your Heart)

Words by William Engvick. Music by Georges Auric

this, I wor - ry and won - der, You're close to me here, but where is your heart? It's a sad thing to re - al - ize that you've a heart that nev - er melts. When we kiss, do you close your

The Girl From Ipanema (Garota De Ipanema)

Original Words by Vinicius De Moraes. Music by Antonio Carlos Jobim. English Words by Norman Gimbel

The Power Of Love

Words & Music by C. deRouge, G. Mende, J. Rush & S. Applegate

1. The whis-pers in the morn-ing
(Verse 2 see block lyric)

of lov-ers sleep - ing tight,

are roll - ing by— like thun - der now—

as I look___ in your eyes.

I hold on___ to your bo - dy,___

and feel each move you make,

your voice is warm and ten - der, a love that

I could _____ not for - sake.

'Cause I'm your la - - dy, _____

and you are my man, _____ when - ev - er you reach _____

for me, I'll do all that I can. _____

Repeat to fade

Verse 2:
Lost is how I'm feeling
Lying in your arms,
When the world outside's too much to take,
That all ends when I'm with you.
Even though there may be times
It seems I'm far away,
Never wonder where I am
'Cause I am always by your side.

(They Long To Be) Close To You

Words by Hal David. Music by Burt Bacharach

139

Those Were The Days

Words & Music by Gene Raskin

Slowly

Once up-on a time there was a ta-vern
Then the bu-sy years went rush-ing by us. We
Just to-night I stood be-fore the ta-vern.
Through the door there came fa-mi-liar laugh-ter. I

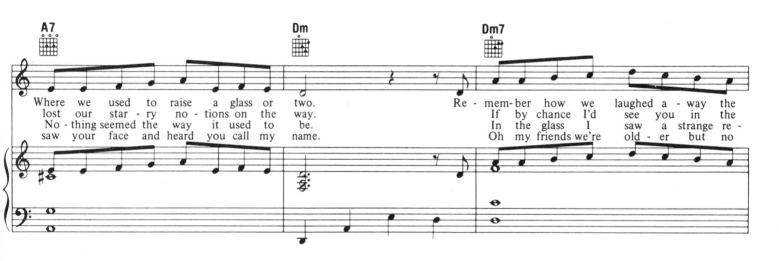

Where we used to raise a glass or two.
lost our star-ry no-tions on the way.
No-thing seemed the way it used to be.
saw your face and heard you call my name.

Re-mem-ber how we laughed a-way the
If by chance I'd see you in the
In the glass I saw a strange re-
Oh my friends we're old-er but no

hours,___ And dreamed of all the great things we would do.
ta-vern, We'd smile at one an-oth-er and we'd say -
flec-tion, Was that lone-ly fel-low real-ly me?
wis-er, For in our hearts the dreams are still the same.

Those Were The
Those Were The
Those Were The
Those Were The

Unchained Melody

Words by Hy Zaret. Music by Alex North

Oh, my love, my dar-ling, I've hun-gered for your touch a long, lone-ly time. Time goes by so slow-ly and time can do so much, Are you still

Wedding March

By Felix Mendelssohn

Allegro vivace (♩ = 144)

Where Do I Begin
(Theme from "Love Story")

Words by Carl Sigman. Music by Francis Lai

love that an-y-where I go _____ I'm nev-er

lone-ly. _____ With her a-long, _____ who could be

lone-ly? _____ I reach for her hand, _____ it's al-ways there. _____

_____ How long does it last? _____ Can love be meas-ured by the

Too Young

Words by Sylvia Dee. Music by Sid Lippman

love. _____ They say that love's a

word, a word we've on - ly heard but

can't be - gin to know the mean - ing of. _____

And yet, we're not too young to

know_____ this love will last though years may go._____ And then some-day they may re-call_____ we were not too young at all. They all.

1.

2.

154

Winter Wonderland

Words by Dick Smith. Music by Felix Bernard

an-y old time, Here in the o-pen, we're walk-in' and hop-in' to-geth-er! ___

Eb   Bb7   Eb   Cm   F7   Bb7   Eb   Fm7 Bb7

CHORUS

Sleigh bells ring, are you list-'nin'! In the lane snow is glist-'nin', A

Lightly   *p–f*

Eb   Bb7   Fm   Bb7

beau-ti-ful sight, We're hap-py to-night, walk-in' in a win-ter won-der-land! Gone a-way is the

F9   Bb7   Eb

blue-bird, Here to stay is a new bird, He sings a love-song, As we go a-long,

Bb7   Fm Bb7

Without You

Words & Music by Peter Ham & Tom Evans

No, I can't for-get this eve-ning, or your face as you were leav-ing, but I guess that's just the way the sto-ry goes. You al-ways smile, but in your eyes your sor-row shows, yes, it shows. ___ No, I can't for-get to-mor-row, when I think of all my sor-row and I

had you there, but then I let you go. And now it's on-ly fair that I should let you

know what you should know: _____ I can't

live, _____ if li-ving is with-out you, _____ I can't live, I can't

give a-ny-more. __ I can't live, _____ if li-ving is with-out you, _____ I can't